Laugier's MARTYRS

a personal analysis

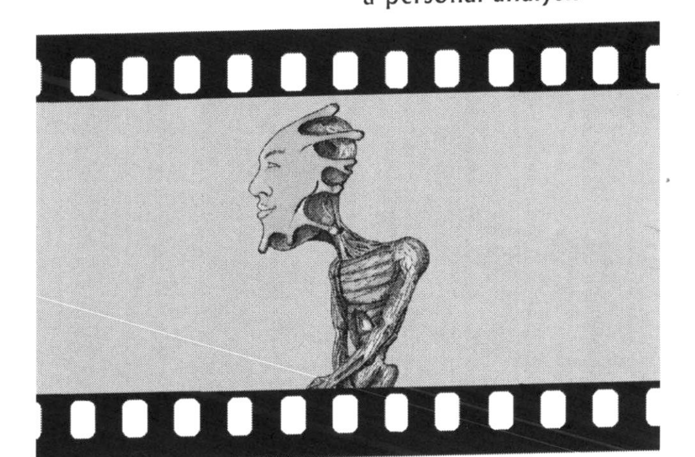

Alex Davis

ROOSTERVISION

Edited by Jeff O'Brien
Cover Design by Nicholas Day, D.F. Noble
RoosterVision logo by Joe Wieneke

Printed in the USA.

www.roosterrepublicpress.com

To Mum – my first horror viewing companion

INTRODUCTION

'If I had thought about it, I would never have made it. I would have worried about what it would do to my career and how people world react to a film like that. I still don't know the answer to that question...'Pascal Laugier, Director of Martyrs

As a horror viewer, and especially a viewer of extreme horror, there are a lot of movies that challenge your boundaries and test what it is you can stand to see portrayed on film. Many are surprising, some genuinely shocking - others give you a palpable sense of nausea.

But for me, the most impactful of movies are those that simply stop you in your tracks. There are only a handful of movies with this sort of power, offerings that put a halt to whatever you had planned for that day and remain with you through the weeks and months that follow. They'll leave you with a sense of deep contemplation, possibly even something akin to depression and melancholy. Put simply, these movies just take some time to *get over*.

I can honestly count films in this bracket on one hand – I was a genuine mess after the screeching, sickening finale of *Thanatomorphose* – one of the most effective pieces of body horror around, in my opinion. I legit cried when the credits rolled on the brutal ending to *Megan is Missing*, probably not the best movie all around but with an absolutely heart-rending closing twenty minutes. It was impossible to concentrate on anything else for the rest of the day. Most recently, *American Guinea Pig: Bloodshock* lived up to its name by leaving me in a complete state of shock, cleverly employing numerous cinematic devices to disturb the viewer to the maximum. Even worse, I had to watch it again the next day for the first UK screening...

But before all those, and the film that first introduced me to this particular effect, was *Martyrs*.

In 2017 it is hard – but not impossible – to still be surprised by a movie. When Martyrs hit back in 2008 I was a member of Blockbuster Video – remember those? - and had a handy branch about ten minute's walk from home, so I'd often stroll down to take a particular look at the horror and world cinema selections. The Ashbourne Road branch of Blockbuster in Derby introduced me to a lot of French cinema, much of which I loved and almost all of which challenged me. I'd been on a rich run of very good movies from the nation – including *In My Skin, Baise-Moi* and the incredible *Irreversible* – which were some of the earlier movies in the New French Extremity movement. And there on the shelf sat *Martyrs*, a movie I knew very little about but very much liked the look of.

Those first viewing of movies that are masterpieces, films that you didn't, *couldn't* possibly have expected to be masterpieces, are moments that you wish you could bottle and open again when you're served up so much of the drivel that horror – particularly in the US – can produce. From the very first scene, *Martyrs* absolutely pinned me to my chair, demanded my attention and did not let it go for a moment for the next 99 minutes. Backing its nightmarish concept with fantastic central performances from Morjana Alaoui and Mylene Jampanoi, and continuing to surprise with each turn of the twisted storyline, this felt like the movie I had been wanting, *needing* for a long time. It helped underpin my earliest ideas of what 'extreme horror' meant and was a key factor in my deciding to explore the subgenre further. For the better part of ten years every film in the field has – in my mind – had this one to live up to.

Many have come close, perhaps one or two have even rivalled it, but nothing has ever truly beaten it.

It's also very telling, the impact this movie has had on other viewers – there are films that you loved that others may pan, or be indifferent to. There are films that divide opinion and draw both love and hate reactions, sparking a superfluity of online debate. This is especially common in extreme horror – it's easy to have an adverse reaction to what can be particularly controversial content. However, everybody I have spoken to about *Martyrs* has offered nothing but praise – in a divisive subgenre, it's a movie that truly unites opinion. Naturally 2016's US remake came in for plenty of flak, again a sign of the esteem and reverence in which the original was held.

Over these pages, we'll be exploring one of the finest pieces of transgressive cinema in the last decade, looking at some of what has made it such an enduring force and the impact it has had on me personally. I doubt very much I would be reviewing and writing about this aspect of cinema today without this one phenomenal movie.

Alex Davis,Derby, December 2016

PROLOGUE

What is it that sets *Martyrs* apart from the crowd? There were three things that personally struck me very strongly about the movie from my many times watching it – firstly, it's very notable the high esteem this movie is held in by the horror community. Rating on websites such as IMDB and Rotten Tomatoes are certainly solid, but it's almost impossible to give this a mention on social media or horror forums without a procession of supporting and positive messages coming in. Given just how negative and critical a place the internet at large can be, that's no mean feat. It's remarkable that even those people who found the movie extremely hard to watch – many firmly refusing to watch a second time, for a host of reasons – still have very kind words about the quality of production, acting and the very concept of the piece.

Secondly, when watching a lot of extreme or transgressive horror, there is a very noticeable trend for movies in that subgenre to focus on one kind of taboo or extremity. That's not to say they can't be brutally effective in delivering that – movies such as

Nekromantik and *Aftermath* take an unflinching look at necrophilia, the first two *Guinea Pig* films presented unremitting torture, *The Human Centipede* and *Thanatomorphose* offer shocking body horror. One of the triumphs of *Martyrs* is that it continues to change throughout, not simply focussing on a single form of taboo but keeping the viewer second-guessing as to what twist or turn will come next. Even more so, it does this in a logical and believable fashion, never becoming a messy melange of shock in the way the works of Marian Dora or even *A Serbian Film* can do. The plot moves along at a pace, often announcing a new chapter or phase with a surprising development or startling moment, and having opened with a bang there's no let-up whatsoever. Again, keeping up this kind of bombardment of the senses can be hard to do without making the viewer feel jaded, or give them the feeling that things are being very much overdone – never does that feel like a factor here.

What else is there that makes *Martyrs* so special? There's doubtless a freshness and originality here, with a plot that explores the psychology of pain, of suffering, tying that into neo-religious elements as well as the mental health damage that can be done by years of torture and abuse. The central performances are also genuinely stunning – Morjana Alaoui as Anna and Mylene Jampanoi in the role of Lucie are both mesmerising, truly committed to the terrible experiences that they are about to endure and have already endured respectively. And – probably most importantly – *Martyrs* eschews the concept of violence, torture and gore as a lowest common denominator, although it certainly doesn't shy away from the brutality innate in its premise. There's no joy taken in the hideous events that unfold, which can so often be the case when budgets are relatively low and there is a desire to shock audiences. So much is presented unflinchingly but – for me – there's no sense of gratuity, of a director, of actors, of an audience getting off on what is presented in any way.

And that's not an easy balance to strike.

THE STORY
PART ONE – LADY VENGEANCE

The first of our two central characters is Lucie, whom we see in the very opening seconds as a young girl, near-naked and fleeing frantically down the street. Battered, bruised and bloodied, this moment leads us into the credits which – dare I say – are slightly clumsy in providing Lucie's background, but equally do save a great deal of time in the main movie itself, allowing us to cover years of exposition in a matter of minutes. Taken into the Assumption Hospital of Pediatric Services, it is discovered that Lucie has been chained for years in a dark room and abused – never raped but regularly deprived of food and drink, beaten and held captive in unhygienic conditions. At the hospital she is withdrawn and lonely, but the credits tell the story of her slowly letting Anna into her world and the two of them becoming fast friends. It's post-credits we are introduced to the unwelcome third wheel in their relationship – a shadowy, unclear and not quite human figure out to terrorise Lucie.

The main thrust of the story takes place

fifteen years later, where we are briefly introduced to a typical French family at breakfast – mum, dad and the two kids discussing school and future plans – before there's a knock on the door. And there stands Lucie, shotgun in hand, who blasts a hole through both the mother and father of the family in no time at all. If this movie hadn't gotten your attention yet, it certainly would do so here – it's a vicious moment that comes from nowhere and is a pure, wake-you-up slap in the face to the viewer. But worse is to come, as Lucie isn't done with mum and dad – she continues on to slaughter both the son and daughter in cold blood. At this stage there's no motive, no explanation for her actions, and this makes the scene all the more shocking.

With this deed of murder done, Lucie goes to the house phone and calls Anna, who is waiting to hear from her. We find out in their conversation that the aim was supposed to be investigation, but obviously Lucie has gone further than that. Anna arrives at the scene, which is a pure bloodbath, and is horrified at what her friend has done. Lucie insists 'it was them' – the people who kidnapped and abused her so long ago – but unsurprisingly Anna has her doubts. However, with all of that said, Anna still stays with her long-time friend and leads the clean-up operation – no mean feat given the clinical execution that has just been carried out. But Anna has an even more important role – looking to protect Lucie from the demon that stalks her...

PART TWO – NEVER FORGIVE, NEVER FORGET

What comes next is a short but vital phase of the movie that says much about Anna and Lucie's relationship, as well as Lucie's mental state. Lucie experiences two attacks from the demon, the corpse-like woman that follows her and launches into brutal violence whenever it sees her. It's a powerful visual and a fine bestial performance to bring it to life so effectively, and for all of Lucie's stern exterior she is obviously mortally afraid of the creature. The first attack happens in a locked bathroom, and Anna is able to break the door down and rescue her friend from the foul being. It is unveiled that this creature is in fact the manifestation of a girl that Lucie was forced to leave behind when making her escape so many years ago – sharply aware that she only had one chance and limited time to gain her freedom, she left her fellow captive behind, something she has never been able to forget or move past the guilt of.

There is a further shock in store when Anna is in another bathroom, looking to dispose of the next body, and the mother of the family – Gabrielle – opens her eyes. This is a moment where the relationship between the two leads truly turns, and the doubts in Anna's mind crystallise. This is not a cruel torturer, in her eyes – this is a woman whose murder was attempted for something she did not do. The doubts in that respect are seeded in the very first scene of the movie proper, in which a much younger Anna claims Lucie can sometimes remember the people who detained and abused her, but she's never been sure. In assisting Gabrielle to escape, she knows she is betraying her old friend, but clearly feels it is morally the right thing to do. When Lucie discovers her looking to help the wounded mother out of the house, she launches into a furious assault, knocking Anna aside and brutally crushing Gabrielle's skull with a hammer. The sense of relief from Lucie is almost palpable – in completing the revenge she sought, she believes that this will exorcise the ghost that has haunted her from those broken early years. Yet the hateful figure appears once again, and this time we see that attack through Anna's eyes for the first time – there's nothing there but a shade of guilt in Lucie's mind. The wounds she inflicts are all her own doing. It's a powerful scene as we cut from a vindictive attack to a tragic instance of self-harm, driven home even further by the realisation from Lucie that there is nothing she can do to put her malevolent spirit to rest. She runs from the house through the front window before using a shard of glass to cut her own throat, the only true end to the life of violence and abuse she can see.

A distraught Anna weeps openly, bringing the body inside and laying it to rest as best she can. She decides to call her mother for some succour – receiving little sympathy from her estranged parent – and while she is on the phone she hears a strange noise from behind the wall...

PART THREE – WHAT LIES BENEATH

Locating the source of the noise, Anna opens a cupboard in one of the main rooms that leads to a strange, sterilised metallic area attached to the house. She investigates further, finding a sub-basement that she can climb to via a long, retractable ladder. And what she finds there makes her rethink everything that has just happened – for in a room deep beneath the house, she finds another victim of horrific torture and abuse. Emaciated, naked, badly scarred, barely able to speak or express herself, this captive is in a truly shocking condition, made even worse by a metallic mask driven into her skull and preventing any light from reaching her. Anna takes it upon herself to help. Dragging the broken woman up to the main house, she gives her a bath – an experience obviously alien to the filthy prisoner – before removing the helmet nailed into the woman's skull. It's a hard scene to watch, as the whole scalp basically peels away with it, and the sunlight is pure agony for the woman. Later, she finds her new companion slicing at her wrists with a knife, grating at skin already worn away and carved at many times in the past. She attempts to stop her from injuring herself further, but we are cut off by another gunshot – one which not only kills this tragic victim, but signals the start of a very dark final chapter for Anna...

PART FOUR – THE UNBROKEN

The house is suddenly full of soldiers dressed in black, and Anna, helpless against the numbers and artillery, finds herself quickly captured and taken down to the basement. There she meets Mademoiselle, an older lady who confirms that the butchered family were indeed Lucie's captors and explains their intentions. We find out little about what the society truly is, or how it functions, but she is part of a sect looking for Martyrs – people who can undergo immense physical and psychological torture. The aim? To get them so close to death that they will see something of what lies beyond the veil. Mademoiselle shows Anna images of the rapt expressions of people in the height of abject pain and near death, and this society wants to know – and are willing to inflict any amount of torment in order to find out. She goes on to explain that women are by far the best subjects for what she calls 'transfiguration' – this is all the warning Anna has before the chloroform rag goes over her face...

She awakens to what is a horrible recapitulation of Lucie's earlier flashbacks. She is strapped to a single seat, hands chained to the armrests, a bucket beneath her by way of a toilet. She is near naked, and uses her first burst of energy in a desperate attempt to escape, but there is no breaking the chains. What follows is – for me –

possibly one of the hardest half-hours in cinema history to watch. *Martyrs* is a film that never flinches, and here it once again doesn't back down from showing the systematic abuse of Anna. She is force-fed an awful-looking yellow gruel, and when she spits it out she is slapped in the face and simply has the spoon crammed into her mouth again. A shadowy male figure comes a number of times, on the first occasion even letting her out of her chains before violently assaulting her, even going so far as to slap her awake after she is unconscious simply to knock her out again with a sucker punch. This man in black returns many times to slap, punch, kick and generally physically break Anna down. Her long hair is cut and shaved, and her initial beauty gives away to a mask of bruises and swelling. As time goes on – and we are given no indication of what time has passed – her will is broken down, bit by bit, signified in part by her final acceptance of the food offered to her. She hallucinates a conversation with Lucie – the bond between the two of them still strong despite it all – before a female visitor tells her that it is nearly all over. There is just one more phase to go through...

Anna is unchained and taken from her cell, and finds herself strapped onto a strange medical apparatus that suspends her, stomach down, before the masked surgeon. It takes a few moments for it to become entirely clear what is going on – Anna is about to be skinned alive. This is probably the only act of violence the movie shies away from in the least, but in leaving this operation to the imagination the shock of seeing Anna in the next scene, flayed clean of all her flesh, is undeniable. It's one of the most brutal visuals in a film absolutely full of them.

Anna has not only survived this final ordeal, but maintains enough of her sanity and her own mind for her to speak – and Mademoiselle is the one to speak to her. All we see is Mademoiselle lean down to her, for Anna to whisper something, before Mademoiselle leaves. It's a great mystery that hangs over the end of this movie – made even greater by the fact that, when the higher-uppers of this strange society arrive, Mademoiselle decides to shoot herself rather than revealing what she has discovered. It's a suitably blunt and impactful finale for a piece loaded with hammer blows, and one that has left audiences debating since *Martyrs* was released.

"Can you imagine what comes after death?" she asks."No." the response comes. "Keep doubting." Those are her final words. The gunshot is just seconds behind.

It's hugely powerful stuff.

We close with a shot closing in on Anna's eyes, and a glimpse of what might lie within them...

ANALYSIS
Anna and Lucie's Relationship

Martyrs is effectively a two-hander. Some other characters appear – Mademoiselle chief among them – but the focus is very much on Lucie and Anna. In the opening scenes of the movie, even as the credits roll, we get a sense of a burgeoning friendship between them in the home they both find themselves in. Anna is finally able to crack through Lucie's shield and gain her confidence and trust. However, it is apparent this is not a trust that extends to anyone else, nor does it signify any great opening up in Lucie's character. Indeed, it is apparent even when we skip to fifteen years and the two of them really don't have anyone else – Lucie calls upon Anna immediately after she has slaughtered the family in the opening scene, and by the time Anna arrives Lucie is almost entirely dependent on her to resolve the matter. Having committed the grisly deed, Lucie seems unable to face up to it. However, it is possible to argue that the relationship is distinctly co-dependent – there is a sense that Anna feels a desperate need to look after and protect Lucie, an overwrought sense of responsibility no doubt built up in their younger years. Children often develop an out-of-proportion sense of things, an enhanced sense of responsibility for what goes on around them, and I feel this is why Anna feels such a strong need to care for Lucie – one of the doctors describes her as a 'mummy' in the first montage, to which Anna replies 'she has no one'. Little moments such as this tell you a lot.

There is possibly another layer to this relationship as well – in the bathroom of the family's house, as the two talk, corpses strewn around them, Anna kisses Lucie. It is something that Anna is obviously committed to as an action, but Lucie's response is merely 'What are you doing?'. It's a moment that has significance but doesn't hang over the movie – there's no need or desire for exploitative sexual tension been the two. Yet perhaps the care for Lucie goes much deeper for Anna, beyond the protective and motherly into the romantic. But there's certainly no sense of that being reciprocated – you could argue that any such romance would be doomed, as Lucie (for me) is a character swallowed by obsessions and deeply wrapped in her own psychoses. She has every right to be troubled, given what she has endured, but her dependence on Anna feels deep and total. It does not seem to be borne out of the same affection or unselfishness – it is a need that is hungry, and what she asks of Anna in the movie time and time again is far beyond what could possibly be expected of even the very closest of friends. Yet Anna is keen to deliver time and time again, and puts herself in deep danger for Lucie.

The moment this shifts is when Anna finds that Gabrielle – the mother of the family – is still alive. Desperate to hide the fact that she has survived, Anna conspires with Gabrielle to get her out of the house and into the woods surrounding it. It's hardly an extensive sort of help, but it is as much as Anna feels she can deliver whilst A) hiding it from her friend and B) not alerting any authorities to what has happened in the short-term. Do these actions constitute a betrayal? Yes and no. To Lucie, these people are terrible human beings who degraded her and ruined her life – an impression that ultimately turns out to be accurate. To Anna, these are innocent victims of her friend's shattered mental state – a revenge targeted in the wrong direction. This is the tipping point in their relationship, and a part of what drives Lucie into the shadowy place that leads to her suicide. The two end up in a physical altercation as Lucie launches her fatal hammer attack on Gabrielle, but interestingly only fights her long-term friend off with her hands. There's no sense she can or would hold the same murderous rage to her friend, even in this circumstance. But left with no true friend to call upon, and no respite from the creature that has haunted her mind for so long, Lucie takes her life – and the last thing that Anna did to her was to traitorously go behind her back and help her tormentors. It's doubtless a sour end to what was a dysfunctional but emotionally powerful friendship.

It's interesting that Anna finds the second (or should that be latest?) victim of the family so soon after, and is again so keen to help. It certainly suggests a compassionate nature on her part – which is on display in many scenes – but is there equally an aspect of deep guilt, or even of transference, on her part? She was unable to save Lucie, despite all her best efforts and years of trying to rescue this beautiful and tragic heroine. But in finding a new captive, she has a second chance to try and save a life, to try and nurse back to both mental and physical health. Maybe this is what makes Anna such a great martyr? She is more than happy to stop her own life – which we truly know nothing of – in order to help someone else in need, to sacrifice her own happiness and wellbeing to try and bring a little of that to another.

In both cases she fails, and it's quite possible that both of the women she tries to save were truly beyond help, making her even more of a tragic character – in her efforts to save others, she ends up in a worse position than them. If you look up the dictionary definition of a martyr - 'a person who is put to death or endures great suffering on behalf of any belief, principle, or cause' – Anna is practically a textbook definition.

What comes across to me in how little background we get on each of the characters – the opening childhood montage being our only real information on them beyond the main narrative of the movie – makes for a fascinating dynamic. All we really know of them is what we see in their interaction – and as such our view of Lucie is deeply affected by Anna's view of her, and behaviour towards her, with the same very much applying to the Anna that we see through Lucie's eyes.

Feminism and Misogyny

Obviously, I write this as a man and can only watch this movie through male eyes, but it would be remiss of me to pass over one of the most common arguments swirling around this movie – is it misogynistic and anti-feminist? It's no easy question to answer, but certainly one that bears some exploration. On the surface it would be easy to say 'yes' – we see three women incarcerated and put through varying degrees of degrading abuse, and none of that is presented with a soft edge. Many of my female friends have expressed varying degrees of disgust at the physical violence meted out upon Anna in the final section of the movie, and rightly so – I don't think anything would claim that's easy to sit through. But would the movie be as effective without it? Would the true nature of the suffering that Anna goes through be underplayed without that? Indeed, would it fit with the tone and style of the rest of the movie if we were to see the camera pan away, or to fade to the next scene? From moment one, *Martyrs* is absolutely in your face, and to me it feels only fitting that it should stay there – it's part of what has made it such an enduring classic of extreme cinema.

If you once again take the dictionary definition of feminism – admitting before time that it is a word that can mean different things to difference people – we have 'the doctrine advocating social, political, and all other rights of women equal to those of men.' And without dispute, women in this movie are subjugated, abused and have their rights routinely taken away through *Martyrs,* with the acts against them committed by both men and women. But when you dig deeper into the motivation behind that within the plot, it's a little more complicated than that.

To take a more general argument of whether women are presented as some way inferior to men in *Martyrs*, I would say certainly not. Lucie is a hardened survivor who has been through awful experiences and come through the other side deeply scarred, but driven by a steely determination to gain revenge on those that made her suffer. Actress Mylene Jampanoi, who plays the role, says 'Lucie is a heroine – she makes progress, she's determined... she wants to get out of the mess she's in.' This was a character who was never going to accept or settle for the captivity that her abusers would have forced upon her, and the fact that she is still standing despite the 'demon' that inflicts hideous wounds upon her time and time again is a testament to her strength of character. She even manages to have her final revenge all these years on from her escape. Anna cares deeply for her friend, and is strong in her own right, more lucid than her counterpart but more than willing to go the extra mile and take on whatever task is required. Pascal Laugier himself described Lucie's strength as 'more direct, more in your face, more sparky', whereas Anna's character is more gentle, but still with plenty of strength when needed. When Anna does find herself captured, we once again see her mental strength on display. Despite all the harrowing attacks visited on her, she is still able to continue on and become the ultimate martyr. To remember the words of Mademoiselle – the female leader of the society behind the movement – 'women are more suited for the transfiguration. Why? Because they are stronger, more resilient, and harder to break.' There's no message here that women are in some way weaker than men – the female characters here endure the extraordinary suffering put before them for longer than anyone could possibly expect. Female captives are chosen not because of hatred for them, or the wish to subjugate, but because they can survive more. It's never said explicitly, but their male counterparts would be destroyed long beforehand.

Even Mademoiselle is a very strong character – clearly a powerful ruler of the society and a strong intellect, her final decision to let the truth of the afterlife die with her could be taken as an act of strength rather than an act of weakness. Of course, without the full context of what she knows, we'll never be able to make a proper assessment of what that action meant – although we will come to that later.

It's not a movie that you could call pro-feminist, but when you start to pull it apart I would consider it unfair to call it anti-feminist. And there are plenty of films out there that would fit that bill – in fact you could argue that extreme cinema has more than any other area of cinema. The more recent French release *Frustre* feels like a prime example, and if you have the stomach to watch any of Lucifer Valentine's work the way that woman are presented and treated in those movies is truly appalling. There are also movies such as Japan's *Tumbling Doll of Flesh* and Argentina's *Snuff 102* that leave a horrible misogynistic taste in the mouth.

Does *Martyrs* revel in its treatment of women? Is there any sense the director has a hatred of his female characters? Is the suffering happening *because* another character hates women? The answer to all of those, for me, would be no – bottom line, I think it's a much smarter movie with far more integrity than that.

Mental Illness

Another issue it is hard to duck in the piece is that of mental illness, and how it is presented here. Lucie is clearly a character suffering from a very specific visual and audio hallucination, which is a manifestation of deep-lying guilt that she left someone else to continue suffering while she made her own escape. You could easily argue that she is being extremely unfair on herself – in the scene where she gets away her window of opportunity is extremely limited, as she manages to injure her captor and fall from her chair in basically a single action. Without any keys or means to release her fellow captor, let alone the fact that there are a second set of footsteps descending the stairs, what else could she have possibly done?

But the mind in an extreme state of distress very rarely works to that sort of logic, at the time or with any kind of hindsight. It's easy to – for a while at least – take the being as real, because it is presented to us as such and the damage that it does is extremely real. If there is a single flaw in the movie – and it pains me to point it out – the first time we see the 'demon' in the main thread of the story, it pins Lucie down before stabbing and raking at her back with a kitchen knife. Given we later know this demon is basically a representation of her own self-harm, I'm not sure how she could inflict such debilitating wounds to her own back, especially from the position she was in. Presumably there is an element of making the creature more believable, but it becomes a little jarring with what we discover later on. Lucie's behaviour would seem to have all the hallmarks of schizophrenia, which of course still has no firm known cause, but environmental factors are certainly a strong influence alongside genetic factors (we of course discover nothing of Lucie's parents of family background). But given the extreme experience and the trauma and mental anguish suffered by Lucie, it would have been hard to escape entirely unscathed. As well as hallucinations, she carries other clear symptoms of schizophrenia – hallucinations we have covered already, but she also suffers from delusions (IE the overblown sense of responsibility for the victim she left behind) and very muddled thoughts. Whilst Lucie has some strong moments of clarity, she often looks somewhat distant or confused in other scenarios. For example, after killing the family in the opening, she seems deeply unsure of what to do next until Anna arrives.

Our opening scenes – throughout the credits – show both Anna and Lucie in what looks like an orphanage, and while it is known to some extent what she goes through she never tells much of her experience. It is unclear what treatment – be it medical or psychological – she was ever given for her condition, but given this phase of the story would have been happening during the 1970s and 1980s it's very likely that understanding of the condition would have been at least a little behind what it is now. Many of the scenes shown in this initial montage seem to be typical of orphanages, so again it's never totally clear if it is a specialist facility of some kind or not. We don't really get enough impression of the other children to make any clear judgement in that respect. There also seems to be little apparent evidence of mental illness in Anna, which also makes me think that perhaps Lucie did not receive suitable treatment and would perhaps explain some of her behaviour fifteen years on.

Our second victim suffers her own hallucination, as revealed by Mademoiselle later in the movie – in this instance the abused suffers visions of cockroaches crawling over her flesh, which she is trying to remove and cut off. In fact, for Mademoiselle, some delusion or 'monster' is so common in people she has tried to martyr that for her it is a matter of fact, something everyday. It's not a movie that demonises mental illness in any way, more a scathing study of what extreme trauma can do to people – indeed you can argue that's the central tenet of *Martyrs*. How could anyone come through months – years – of mental torture and emerge unscathed?

It is possible to argue that even Anna – while she remains remarkably strong for a long time in the face of her own ordeal – finally gives in to auditory hallucinations in her final conversation with Lucie, taking place in her head. You may want to take an optimistic view that she is somehow communicating beyond the grave, but more likely that Anna is looking to find some kind of solace in her situation – and will happily accept an imagined moment of relief. Indeed, it's all she is liable to find.

Mademoiselle – And The Whisper

The third main character in the movie – if there can be considered to be one – is Mademoiselle. The one extensive scene featuring her – in which she talks to Anna about the society and the very idea of martyrdom – is extremely telling. 'It's so easy to create a victim', she says. 'You lock someone in a dark room. They begin to suffer. You feed that suffering, methodically, systematically and coldly. And make it last.' And that is exactly what all three of our female protagonists are – victims, people who have all suffered at the hands of a society so bent on its ends that they will simply do anything to get there. Lucie is the only one who is ever able to strike back, to move away from being a victim and become an aggressor, to place the shoe on the other foot.

In the scene mentioned above, Mademoiselle references their attempts to use children – and we know what Lucie endured in her younger days. Just how deep and how wide does the society run? How many members are there? How many women does it have locked up and suffering abjectly? How is it funded and organised? Again, these are questions that we get – at best – a glimpse of the answers to. In the final scene, we see plenty of very expensive cars, suggesting this society has plenty of people involved with both money and influence. The people are dressed remarkably similarly, suggesting perhaps strong traditions or strict rules. Beyond that – who is Mademoiselle? Who are any of the other people involved? How could such a thing be kept secret for so long? These are all conundrums that are beyond us to solve.

Yet Mademoiselle's certainty of the hallucination and delusion suffered by her martyrs does beg a further question – namely, even if anyone could tell you what they have seen (which Anna is able to do in the finale) how much can you truly believe it? Could their visions of the afterlife, of what lies beyond death, be yet another symptom of psychoses? If Mademoiselle is so happy to admit that the people they attempt to martyr all suffer some form of hallucination, then could that purported glimpse of the afterlife be just another delusion? It adds another tantalising angle to the puzzle that is the end of this movie – whatever Mademoiselle was told, did she believe it? And if so, should she have believed it? Is her killing herself the right thing to do, or the wrong thing to do? Is she moving on to a better world, or does she simply want whatever knowledge she has to end with her? Was what she was told so traumatic?

That moment – what it is that Anna tells Mademoiselle – remains a hot topic of discussion around Martyrs, and again bears some sort of explanation. There are two ways that it could be taken – firstly, that what Anna passes on sounds so wonderful and paradisiacal that Mademoiselle simply cannot wait to get there, hence committing suicide in the finale. However, if this were the case, would this not be joyous news she would want to pass on before taking her last steps to this promised land after death? Or does she have some concern that the society will all want to follow that route, giving up their work – and what could conceivably be her life's work – and ending itself in the process?

However, in my own opinion, I think that Anna simply passes on that there is nothing there in the afterlife at all. In the scenes where we do zoom in closely on Anna's eyes after she is flensed, we don't see anything we could recognise as clear religious imagery – however there is a sense of stars, and space, and infinity. That's speculative, of course, but there are two things to me that speak more clearly to this interpretation – firstly, the fact that Mademoiselle decides that suicide is a suitable step. Many religions are of course firmly against suicide, and claim it is a clear barrier to the more positive aspects of the afterlife. If Mademoiselle holds any religious beliefs – and again this is never utterly clear – then surely she would be of the opinion that killing herself would bar her from heaven, or any other paradise or nirvana? It's also a very strong reaction, but the reaction of a strong woman in order to keep something awful a secret – she has discovered something her society has wanted to know for a long time, and the chances of her even leaving the house without having to pass on that revelation are none. A huge number of members of the society have arrived upon discovering the news of Anna's insight – Mademoiselle can scarcely walk out and not tell them. So she does the only thing she can think of to keep what she knows a secret – allowing the secret to die with her.

We also have that final line of dialogue – 'keep doubting'. It clearly indicates that Mademoiselle does not want to pass on whatever clarity she has, and that now that she knows the answer it is something that could not, should not be known. In finding out the answer to the biggest question humanity has ever had, she realises that she has gone too far, that the human mind simply cannot compute the answer or live on in its knowledge. The significance of doubt – taken as a polar opposite of belief – is that we never can know the answer. You can hold a religion to your heart as a profound belief, but in the end you could be wrong.

Imagine if the revelation that there is nothing after death were to be made public, with proof positive? All religion around the world would be irreparably damaged, and even those without religion could use it as ground to let their most awful, basest instincts out. After all, if there's no cosmic or eternal punishment waiting for bad behaviour, and no everlasting award for good behaviour, many people would use that as a basis to simply do what they like.

Religion

The subheading there might be something of a misnomer, because there's no deep religious angle at the heart of the movie. With a title like *Martyrs* – a term so often bandied around in a religious context – you'd be forgiven for looking for it all the way through. The term is of course often associated with dying for or suffering for religious beliefs, but it can be applied to belief or principles of any kind. Even the other term that Mademoiselle uses – 'transfiguration' – is loaded with religious connotations. Two of its four definitions are 'the supernatural and glorified change in the appearance of Jesus on the mountain. Matt. 17:1–9' and 'the church festival commemorating this, observed on August 6', although in both those instances it would carry a capital letter. You can consider those loaded terms, but beyond that what do we have? There's little to no other religious reference anywhere in the movie. The bodies of the dead are not given any kind of religious burial or rites, but simply dumped unceremoniously in a hole in the ground. I can't recall a single reference to god or any other deity in the context of *Martyrs*.

Indeed, the religious debate above around the finale is much more in my own mind as a viewer than it ever is on screen.

The religious issue was perhaps a little more prevalent in the US remake of 2015 – which has probably been the elephant in the room throughout this book – with the movie's poster going so far as making a cross out of the 'T', with a sharp point going towards a woman's eye. But there's also one scene in said remake with distinct religious connotations, with a woman being nailed to a cross before being burned alive. Make of that what you will – maybe America has a wider obsession or a stronger relationship with religion – but personally I don't take Martyrs as a story about religion. It is a story about struggle, about revenge, about survival, about the terrible impact of trauma, but not one offering any true comment on religion. Indeed, the curiosity of what comes after death does not have to be an implicitly religious question. An atheist will heartily believe there is nothing after that, whereas an agnostic will have an open mind without holding any strong view or belief of what that might be. Indeed, even if your curiosity on the subject comes from a religion, every religion differs to some extent on what the answer to that question is. And to go a leap further – even someone with a scientific bent could have an interest in that same subject, although the most coldly logical may say 'obviously it can only be nothing'.

The end of the movie is not to suggest that it is unknowable – *Martyrs* offers up one very extreme method to find an answer to that biggest of all questions – but the finale perhaps better expresses that it's something that *shouldn't* be known by people. It also begs the question of what the society/sect/cult/movement – call it what you will – can do next after the loss of their leader and such vital, life-changing information slipping away from them. The final shot is designed to establish that Anna is too far gone to share her revelation a second time. Would it be something that galvanises their need to know, or would the loss of that revelation be too devastating for the group to get over?

Making a Martyr – Exploring Suffering

One of the aspects of the movie that fascinated me the most was the process of a person being martyred, as it is seen by the society that makes it happen. We have glimpses of this in Lucie's flashbacks, and a further insight into this when Anna discovers the latest victim, but of course we get our deepest look into this when Anna herself is imprisoned and subjected to the process of humiliation and degradation in detail. There has long been a sort of theory about creative people that they are at their best when they are unhappy, or more precisely that will be the time they produce their best work – Edgar Allan Poe, one of the great Gothic writers, lived a life loaded with dark events and tragedy to provide plenty of fodder for his masterworks. You could view the concept of *Martyrs* as an extension of that – only in suffering and misery are we able to provide genuine, cutting insight, and only in the deepest pits of pain can we dream to answer some of the most fundamental questions of humanity.

But what is it about Anna that makes her such an incredible martyr, and what is it about women that the society believes makes them such good candidates for 'transfiguration'? What little we see of Lucie in her flashbacks suggests that she simply had too much strength of will to be the martyr that the society wanted – in each flashback scene there is a fight, there is grim resistance, and in making an escape she effectively does something that (we assume as viewers) no one else has done in that time. Even Mademoiselle implies they were sloppy and unprofessional to let her escape, but concedes that Lucie finding her captors fifteen years on is no mean feat. The refusal to be broken is probably a key concept for a 'martyr' in the wider sense, but in the sense this movie takes the word you could argue it is a negative. People who continue fighting and continue fighting are not suitable for their purpose. Fight and resistance are natural, but a person can only be 'transfigured' by the ultimate loss of hope and indeed the acceptance of suffering. The final montage of the movie – where we see a condensed version of all Anna's respective hardships – is extremely difficult viewing, and it's hard to be surprised that her willpower is finally crushed under the continual assault.

You could equally argue that the society's belief in the process and what they base their theory upon is pretty flimsy. When Mademoiselle and Anna talk – or more Mademoiselle talks at Anna – she shows her a range of photos of people in extreme suffering and asks her to observe the look in their eyes. Admittedly these photos are taken over a wide range of time, and in the moment are a powerful device. But as a means to justify such barbarism and brutality, a few people with a similar far-gone look in their eyes is not the strongest of reasoning. Does that hint at an underlying, unmentioned religious agenda, a deeper belief in the society that may transcend rational evidence? Or is Mademoiselle simply a charismatic leader who draws people to her and infectiously passes her personal belief to them?

Also, to catch on again to that tricky definition of 'martyr' – none of the prisoners of this society are really suffering or dying for their own beliefs. They are 'victims', they are caught in something they cannot escape from. Fundamentally, they are dying for *someone else's* beliefs – the belief that, at the end of a long tunnel of suffering, is some sort of message from a realm beyond our own. None were asked and none volunteered. If the members of the society believed in their own words so much, would they not allow themselves to be the recipients of these foul experiments and – maybe – reap the profound results? A true believer in a cause such as this, you could argue, would potentially be willing to put themselves forward. Then again, maybe they place an equal importance of what it is to be able to cause suffering, the right kind of suffering – to have the stomach and the stoniness of heart required to truly hurt someone to get what you want. Pascal Laugier provides a slightly disturbing parallel in the way the movie is made, in telling just how hard it was to keep the actresses involved so upset and crying so much on set – effectively a requirement for either of them to effectively deliver their parts. In his own words, Laugier had to 'overcome some of his inhibitions' and ask Jampanoi and Alaoui to hurt themselves in order to keep the tears flowing – making them almost martyrs to the project itself. It's an extreme form of method acting for sure, although sadly you have to say it's anything but unheard of in extreme horror and indeed more mainstream pieces.

While we rarely see the members of the society in action, we have to remind ourselves that these are people who are, quite simply, morally reprehensible. The opening scene in which Gabrielle and her husband and their kids are offered up as a typical, happy French family is very much an illusion designed to throw you off as a viewer. As the story plays out, we discover that Lucie was on to them and that Anna had fallen for the perfect image presented. Without the context provided later, in those opening scenes we feel sympathy for two people who are effectively monsters. The people we do keep and maintain sympathy for are their kids, who likely had no idea what was going on under their very noses and are, in their own way, victims of what is playing out around them.

And when the larger group of society members arrive in droves at the end of the movie, looking the very picture of respectability, we have to remind ourselves that these people are every bit as bad. Many may not be delivering the torture themselves – the implication is that these are kind of dignitaries, but enablers of this sort of behaviour are surely no better than those carrying it out, especially if that enabling is knowingly and willingly carried out? They're not willing to suffer, or even to get their hands dirty – all they want is the rewards that can bring. Maybe there's a strange analogy for capitalism in there somewhere...

Gratuity

Another accusation sometimes levelled at this film – and one that I would strongly refute – is that the violence and bloodshed presented are gratuitous. The idea of gratuity is of course a personal one, and you may feel very differently than me on this issue. Having watched an awful lot of extreme horror, I'd say there were some – perhaps even plenty – that do cross that line, with 'shock' elements feeling unnecessary, unjustified or simply overdone. When you are seeking to get a reaction from your audience – and much extreme cinema angles for an extreme reaction – it can be easy to do for a filmmaker. In this case, I think Pascal Laugier is justified in his decisions. It's very noticeable in the making of documentary that the term 'reality' comes up many times – there's no desire to make anything look like an effect, or show off how cleverly things have been put together. There's a drive to make everything look real and believable, even the demon that haunts Lucie – very twisted and broken but also very much human at heart. That, for me, is not a director seeking to shock with gratuity, but looking to deliver a story with impact and extract the maximum impact from the visual aspect of it.

The question of gratuity for me is always 'does the plot need this to be there?' As such, the line for what is gratuitous and what is not moves around from film to film. What could be seen as exploitative or superfluous in one movie might seem perfectly in place in another. A single scene of excessive sex, violence or other taboo activity in a movie could be extremely jarring if there hasn't been much before, or if the remainder has all been off camera. However, done well, that single scene could pack a serious punch – but only if it is not there purely for surprise or shock value.

What *Martyrs* does in its very opening scene is to set itself a benchmark. We have a girl, deeply wounded and injured, running down the street in a bid to escape something. That takes us aback somewhat as a viewer. Two scenes later, a man opens the front door to be shot in the stomach with a shotgun by a young woman who proceeds to kill the entirety of the family. After that, what *could* be considered gratuitous? There's no soft build, no false impressions whatsoever. Shortly after that, we have the first attack from the demon that haunts Lucie – again, the tone is set that there will be blood and their will be violence, and we will not be shirking that issue. Also, what the opening does is set up that this is a very extreme and very dark scenario – as well it should be, given the gravity of what we know has happened. If you are in any way appalled or offended by the first fifteen to twenty minutes, your best bet is probably to turn it off, because it's not liable to get any rosier. *Martyrs* does not let the foot off the accelerator for a moment.

I think *Martyrs* is one of those rare films that is also very much enhanced by not (if you'll pardon the pun) pulling any punches. In every instance that we encounter something violent or something extreme, there is an immediate emotional reaction. Laugier said that 'I wanted the audience to have a gut reaction to what they saw... to be physically affected.' And he might just have achieved it. As a whole, the movie is absolutely harrowing to watch. I know many, many people who have watched it once that stoically refuse to watch it again, sometimes pointing to individual moments that were simply too much or went too far for them personally. That's entirely valid – equally, I know many people who wouldn't touch this movie knowing what they know about it. The journey that the characters go on is not simply for you to watch from a comfortable remove – *Martyrs* endeavours to put you right there from the very get go. If the characters are going through it, then you are going to go through it vicariously. Lucie doesn't get to look away or dodge the issue. Neither does Anna. So why should the viewer be afforded the privilege? These are characters that we come to invest in, and to care about, and to see them suffering is awful. And in a way, even though that may be harder to watch, that's a big part of what moves it away from gratuity. If this were simply two random women we knew nothing about, then maybe you could claim the level of violence and abuse were unnecessary – but is is a key part of both Anna and Lucie's journey and respective character arcs.

The response to the remake was very telling in this respect. Even the scriptwriter, Mark L Smith, admitted that he wrote much of the violence to be implied or 'off screen' because that was how he preferred it. Again, that's a legitimate feeling if that's how you like your horror. But in taking that out, you lose so much of the impact of *Martyrs*. With a storyline that is pretty close to the original – at least for more than half the feature – why does the French version have such a huge cult following while the Hollywood version is so widely lamented? You can't necessarily put that all on the unflinching nature of the French version, but it's undoubtedly a factor. In removing that, the US version felt very sanitised and watered down. Of course there's plenty of other reasons the French is better to boot – superior acting performances, better visuals and direction, a much sharper ending...

LEGACY
The Remake

And since I have brought it up, I probably have to address it in more detail. The negotiations and thought process for a US remake of *Martyrs* seem to go back even to 2008, the year the original was released, so for it only to emerge in 2015 does tell of a somewhat difficult journey to the screen. The project changed directors after the original choice, Daniel Stamm, was advised by his agent not to take the movie on and so the film arrived with eventual directors The Goetz Brothers. Without wishing to get into my now traditional Blumhouse rant, their name next to a movie is anything but an endorsement for me, and this again proved to be the case.

Many people questioned what an American remake – aimed at a larger market – would really bring. There were concerns that the movie would be substantially toned down, fears that were realised in the final analysis. Not only was much of the violence toned down, but the second half of the new version veered away substantially from the original. After 30-45 minutes I was still feeling reasonably warm towards this new version, but with the 'second victim' in the basement being a little girl, the deviations began and the ending added a new element of hope to the story. And while that may work better for a Hollywood/mainstream cinema audience it removed an awful lot of what made the original so effective.

The *Martyrs* remake did get a serious critical panning, and was generally seen in a very negative light by fans of the original – although that's a statement that holds true for many a movie. I think what made this so galling is that there was never really any way this *would* work well – bringing a brutal slice of French Extremity and attempting to adapt it for a horror audience used to much tamer fare always looked like a recipe for disaster. Even though both were certified 18, much of the visceral, gut punch of the French was lost in the US version.

In my view, the US take isn't necessarily a bad movie in its own right. In my original review, I awarded it 6.5 out of 10 and said 'It's not brilliant, and it no doubt lacks the raw intensity of the French, yet there is enough to keep a viewer interested.' But equally, why would you watch a 6.5/10 when there's a 10/10 out there? Would that summary review tempt you in as much as this from my take on the original – 'The French extreme scene put out plenty more good and even very good movies, but nothing for me ever matched this one. Simply unmissable.'

Beyond the question of 'is the remake any

good?' there's a more telling question: 'was there any point to a remake?'

New French Extremity

French cinema, in my personal opinion, is very much a national product that has two sides. There can be a much softer, lighter, romantic side to films from the nation – Jampanoi said that in other French films she would be playing 'a cute little thing' – while there are also a number of very good, taut crime and thriller movies. But until around 2000, it wasn't necessarily a place that I considered to be a home for great extreme movies. Yet it was around the turn of the century that we started to see a great wave of exciting new movies from France that were pushing boundaries, few of which were flat-out horror but all of which were challenging, transgressive viewing. This movement became known as the New French Extremity and – as an ardent fan and reviewer of extreme cinema – it's something that I am immensely grateful for.

Back in the introduction I mentioned a few films that were considered part of this movement – *Baise-Moi* was one of the first movies to introduce flatly pornographic content to a larger audience (I hesitate to use the term 'mainstream audience') and featured two porn actresses in its lead. *Irreversible* challenged conventional storytelling by starting at the end of the tale – with what would have been a crunching finale in its own right – and working backwards to a revelation that makes what we know is to come even more startling. It also features one of the most horrible rape scenes ever filmed, in my opinion. *In My Skin* showed graphic scenes of self-abuse and cutting and remains one of the toughest films I've ever put myself through as a viewer. *Ma Mere* was a frank look at incest – probably one of the last true cinematic taboos in modern society. Other films in the movement well worth a look are *Sheitan* (starring the never less than brilliant Vincent Cassel), *Frontieres, Trouble Every Day* and the multi-titled *Haute Tension/Switchblade Romance*.

At the time, which I can recall pretty well, it felt like we were right in the middle of something very exciting, a new wave of cinema that would not only sweep over Europe but perhaps even go further than that. Nothing in cinema excites me more than something daring, something challenging, and one film after another from France brought with it fresh risks, fresh style and fresh – if I dare use the word – *danger* for the viewer. I'd never bought into French cinema that much before, but for the first half of the 2000's I was keeping an eagle-eyed watch on anything bursting from the nation.

However, it's probably fair to say that the New French Extremity was ultimately pretty short-lived and hasn't really had the legacy that we might have hoped. *Martyrs* is a relatively late entry into that canon – having been released in 2008 – and you could argue a suitable coda to a range of films that were genuinely exciting to watch, and nothing like anything you'd encountered before. It's even fair to say that the output of the directors that started to emerge in that time has turned out to be pretty disappointing. To take Pascal Laugier, director of *Martyrs*, as one example, his only work since has been the serviceable but not spectacular US horror movie *The Tall Man*, starring Jessica Biel. A new feature, *Incident in a Ghost Land*, will be coming later in 2017. Gaspar Noe has only made two features since 2002's *Irreversible*, although *Enter The Void* is certainly well worthy of mention here. Alexandre Aja (of *Haute Tension*) is arguably the director to have gone onto the most mainstream/Hollywood success, directing the remake of *The Hills Have Eyes* as well as new features such as *Mirrors* and *Horns*. However, directing *Piranha 3D* was perhaps a much lower point...

It's possible that as the movement began to run out of steam as we came towards the new decade of 2010 that some of these very talented directors – Laugier included – found the kind of work they wanted to produce falling out of vogue and as such had to make difficult adaptations to new branches of cinema, or equally found it harder to secure support and funding for new original features. Laugier has publicly lamented the attitude of the French cinema industry towards horror, saying that horror directors 'accused of something we're not guilty off' –

namely making bad movies. Personally I find it hard to fault the overall quality of horror movies coming out of France, but obviously the feeling within the nation itself is different. *Martyrs* has certainly had great international appeal and success regardless.

Either way, the movement died off pretty quickly and while there is doubtless a great body of work left behind, whether the New French Extremity truly had the impact expected remains very much up for debate.

CONCLUSION

For me, my approach to talking about and reviewing film remains intensely personal, because extreme horror and extreme cinema is something that I have a deep passion for. I'm constantly looking out for new movies and new directors, and when I discover something that I think is very good I do have the habit of getting rather evangelical over it.

That's because – with all due respect to the genre – extreme cinema isn't a genre that produces consistent quality. I've written about this before elsewhere, but there are hardcore gorehounds out there who will happily settle for plenty of blood, violence and sex without really having a quality plot or good performances to back them up. If that's your bag, then fair enough, and you're liable to be pretty well serviced by the current film industry. I certainly wouldn't censor or deprive anyone of what they enjoy. But as someone who's been involved working in writing for long past a decade also, I care a lot about story, and characters, and structure – things that can get overlooked when budgets are low and pressures on all involved in a film's production are high. And if you can make a film that has an audience, then why wouldn't you? I get the reasons behind it, but it can mean that the genre I love the most doesn't always sit well with me.

You can hear a lot of buzz and a lot of fuss about a movie and then simply wind up thinking, *that was just shock for shock value*. One of my biggest disappointments of last year was the much-vaunted *The Green Inferno*, supposedly so hard to watch that people were fainting away in cinemas. On viewing, not only was it not very horrific or shocking, but huge elements of it were nothing but laughable. Extreme cinema, when it is presented with *real* quality, and artistry, and emotional impact, is simply one of the finest things around. And those moments of joy at finding something so special and so unforgettable makes up for any number of movies that miss the mark.

There are many films that his fit this bill, but chief among them stands *Martyrs*. This is a movie that has an edge of reality, and has power and passion, and doubtless has huge impact – it's not a movie to watch and forget about easily. You can feel the endeavour and the commitment from all involved in every shot. It's no easy ride, but this is cinema at its most rewarding – deep, complex, challenging, taut, wonderfully acted and original. Next year will see the movie's tenth anniversary and – hopefully – we'll see a well-deserved resurgence and new appreciation for a film that may have passed many horror viewers by.

THANKS

I want to extend a grateful thanks to a handful of great people:

Jim McLeod, 'The Don' of the wonderful Ginger Nuts of Horror, for giving me the chance to explore extreme cinema more than ever and providing such a great place to share my reviews and interviews.

Chris Kelso, for giving me the chance to write about one of my favourite films at length. It's been an absolute pleasure going back to it.

Jonathan Butcher, who provided such valuable feedback and advice on the project. If you love reading as well as watching extreme horror, you should be reading him for sure.

ACKNOWLEDGEMENTS AND NOTES

All the dictionary definitions found in this book are lifted from www.dictionary.com. It's just my 'go to' online!

Quotes from the director and performers are largely taken from Richard Grandpierre's Making of *Martyrs* feature, *Chroniques Organiques*, which is featured on many of the DVD releases of the original movie. There are also some featured in Laugier's 2008 interview with www.filmsactu.com, again found on some DVD releases.

For reference, here is a full list of the other films mentioned within this book, with a little more information provided to make them easier to find. I've organised them below alphabetically:Aftermath (Dir. Nacho Cerda, Spain, 1994)American Guinea Pig: Bloodshock (Dir. Marcus Koch, USA, 2016)Baise-Moi (Dir. Virginie Despentes and Coralie, France, 2000)Enter The Void (Dir. Gaspar Noe, France/Germany/Italy/Canada, 2009)Frontieres (Dir. Xavier Gens, France/Switzerland, 2007)Frustre (Dir. Jacques Vendome, France, 2013)Guinea Pig: The Devil's Experiment (Dir. Saturo Ogura, Japan, 1985)
Guinea Pig: Flower of Flesh and Blood (Dir. Saturo Ogura, Japan, 1985)Haute Tension (or Switchblade Romance)Horns (Dir. Alexandre Aja, USA/Canada, 2013)In My Skin (Dir.

Marina de Van, France, 2002)Irreversible (Dir. Gaspar Noe, France, 2002)Ma Mere (Dir. Christophe Honore, France/Portugal/Austria/Spain, 2004)Megan is Missing (Dir. Michael Goi, USA, 2011)Mirrors (Dir. Alexandre Aja, USA/Romania/Germany, 2008)Piranha 3D (Dir. Alexandre Aja, USA, 2010)Sheitan (Dir. Kim Chapiron, France, 2006)Snuff 102 (Dir. Mariano Peralta, Argentina, 2007)Thanatomorphose (Dir. Eric Falardeau, Canada, 2012)The Green Inferno (Dir. Eli Roth, USA/Canada/Chile, 2013)The Hills Have Eyes (Dir. Alexandre Aja, USA, 2006)The Human Centipede (Dir. Tom Six, Holland, 2009)The Tall Man (Dir. Pascal Laugier, USA/Canada/France, 2012)Trouble Every Day (Dir. Claire Denis, France/Germany/Japan, 2001)Tumbling Doll of Flesh (or Niku Daruma) (Dir. Tamakichi Anaru, Japan, 1998)

ABOUT THE AUTHOR

Alex Davis is a writer, events organiser and tutor. A long-time horror fan, he turned his hand to movie reviews for the first time with Film Gutter at the Ginger Nuts of Horror website in January 2015, beginning with the obscure Marian Dora feature *Debris Documentar*. Since then, he has reviewed well over 100 extreme horror movies and interviewed directors and actors in the field including Stephen Biro, Uwe Boll, Eric Falardeau, Dieter Laser, Pollyanna McIntosh, Tom Six, Phil Stevens, Jimmy Weber and Ashley C Williams. This is his first published book on horror cinema.

To find out more about Film Gutter, and to read new content each Thursday, visit http://www.gingernutsofhorror.com/film-gutter.html

Made in the USA
Columbia, SC
04 July 2017